Jack Russell Terrier as Pets

Everything You Need to Know about
Jack Russell Terriers

Jack Russell Terrier Characteristics, Health, Diet,
Breeding, Types, Care and a whole lot more!

By Lolly Brown

Foreword

When you see a dominantly white colored dog with a few patches in the eyes and face having an athletic, strong and energetic personality that is most certainly a Jack Russell Terrier. This breed will be easily seen in a pack of dogs because of its being dominating but at the same time having a friendly disposition.

Jack Russell Terriers were bred to be hunting dogs which makes them a dependable pet because of their natural protective instinct. This breed may be active, agile and athletic but they can also be show dogs because they are recognized by the Jack Russell Terrier Club of America but not the American Kennel Club.

This breed is generally healthy most especially when given the proper nutrition, training and care that they need. Training this breed may be a bit challenging at first but it will be a rewarding experience.

Be more excited in learning more about the Jack Russell Terrier and you might decide to own one while reading through this book.

Table of Contents

Introduction

Roger Caras, a photographer and a writer once said that, "Dogs are not our whole lives, but they make our lives whole." Owning a dog does not only come in to our lives as pets, but they come in to our lives as a lifetime companion. They have the ability to influence our lives and make them as happy as ever. Jack Russell Terrier is one of the dog breeds that would certainly make your life whole. This breed is known to be an active, agile, and intelligent in nature. This breed was made especially for fox hunting that is why they are naturally athletic and trainable.

Jack Russell Terriers are often called JRT's for short. They are one of the many types of the Terrier species. Other terrier species are; Yorkshire Terrier, Bull Terrier, West Highland White Terrier, Boston Terrier, Scottish Terrier, White Hair fox Terrier, Smooth Fox Terrier, Brazilian Terrier and so many more. Having so much terrier species, the JRT does certainly have a unique characteristic that sets it above the rest.

As a pet owner, you must be aware that having a dog also means that you are willing to provide for the needs that they have. The expenses are not a joke because regardless of what breed it is, they need to be well taken care of in terms of nutrition, grooming and most especially their health. As a pet owner, it is not just about investing a significant amount of money into your pet, but also an effort to care and love them wholeheartedly.

JRT's are generally low maintenance dogs and do not require a lot of grooming as compared to the other breeds. What this breed needs is a significant amount of play time and exercise for them to channel out their energy and their natural athletic capabilities. Jack Russell Terriers constantly shed but this can be regulated by brushing their coat often.

This breed is very dependable when it comes to being a watch dog because it is very protective of their owners when an intruder is around. They have barking tendencies because of this. What is important to know about this breed is that they would work well with people who have previously owned a dog. It will take a lot of effort for a first time dog owner to train this kind of breed because of its personality. A good amount of patience is needed to be able to train JRT's but of course, it will worth it.

Before getting a pet, you must be able to get to know the type of dog you will be getting. This book will help you in to getting to know a Jack Russell Terrier better. It will give you useful and helpful tips in taking care, training, feeding, socializing and dealing with them. It will also give you the benefits that you can have as a pet owner of having a pet such as this.

This book also includes information about showing your JRT and even the health problems that an owner will commonly encounter in this type of breed and how to deal with it. I am sure you are excited to get to know more about the Jack Russell Terrier breed, so read on!

Glossary of Dog Terms

AKC – American Kennel Club, the largest purebred dog registry in the United States

Almond Eye – Referring to an elongated eye shape rather than a rounded shape

Apple Head – A round-shaped skull

Balance – A show term referring to all of the parts of the dog, both moving and standing, which produce a harmonious image

Beard – Long, thick hair on the dog's underjaw

Best in Show – An award given to the only undefeated dog left standing at the end of judging

Bitch – A female dog

Bite – The position of the upper and lower teeth when the dog's jaws are closed; positions include level, undershot, scissors, or overshot

Blaze – A white stripe running down the center of the face between the eyes

Board – To house, feed, and care for a dog for a fee

Breed – A domestic race of dogs having a common gene pool and characterized appearance/function

Breed Standard – A published document describing the look, movement, and behavior of the perfect specimen of a particular breed

Buff – An off-white to gold coloring

Clip – A method of trimming the coat in some breeds

Coat – The hair covering of a dog; some breeds have two coats, and outer coat and undercoat; also known as a double coat. Examples of breeds with double coats include German Shepherd, Siberian Husky, Akita, etc.

Condition – The health of the dog as shown by its skin, coat, behavior, and general appearance

Crate – A container used to house and transport dogs; also called a cage or kennel

Crossbreed (Hybrid) – A dog having a sire and dam of two different breeds; cannot be registered with the AKC

Dam (bitch) – The female parent of a dog;

Dock – To shorten the tail of a dog by surgically removing the end part of the tail.

Double Coat – Having an outer weather-resistant coat and a soft, waterproof coat for warmth; see above.

Drop Ear – An ear in which the tip of the ear folds over and hangs down; not prick or erect

Entropion – A genetic disorder resulting in the upper or lower eyelid turning in

Fancier – A person who is especially interested in a particular breed or dog sport

Fawn – A red-yellow hue of brown

Feathering – A long fringe of hair on the ears, tail, legs, or body of a dog

Groom – To brush, trim, comb or otherwise make a dog's coat neat in appearance

Heel – To command a dog to stay close by its owner's side

Hip Dysplasia – A condition characterized by the abnormal formation of the hip joint

Inbreeding – The breeding of two closely related dogs of one breed

Kennel – A building or enclosure where dogs are kept

Litter – A group of puppies born at one time

Markings – A contrasting color or pattern on a dog's coat

Mask – Dark shading on the dog's foreface

Mate – To breed a dog and a bitch

Neuter – To castrate a male dog or spay a female dog

Pads – The tough, shock-absorbent skin on the bottom of a dog's foot

Parti-Color – A coloration of a dog's coat consisting of two or more definite, well-broken colors; one of the colors must be white

Pedigree – The written record of a dog's genealogy going back three generations or more

Pied – A coloration on a dog consisting of patches of white and another color

Prick Ear – Ear that is carried erect, usually pointed at the tip of the ear

Puppy – A dog under 12 months of age

Purebred – A dog whose sire and dam belong to the same breed and who are of unmixed descent

Saddle – Colored markings in the shape of a saddle over the back; colors may vary

Shedding – The natural process whereby old hair falls off the dog's body as it is replaced by new hair growth.

Sire – The male parent of a dog

Smooth Coat – Short hair that is close-lying

Spay – The surgery to remove a female dog's ovaries, rendering her incapable of breeding

Trim – To groom a dog's coat by plucking or clipping

Undercoat – The soft, short coat typically concealed by a longer outer coat

Wean – The process through which puppies transition from subsisting on their mother's milk to eating solid food

Whelping – The act of birthing a litter of puppies

Chapter One: Understanding Jack Russell Terrier

The Jack Russell Terrier breed is AKC recognized. Since it is a recognized breed, it has certain physical characteristics that must pass the given standard. JRT's are expected to have a height proportioned to the body length and the head. This breed is also known as being tough-looking which makes it a compact breed.

This breed is known as active and athletic, but of course that is not the only thing that describes it.

They are also loyal, cheerful and spirited. They are intelligent and they enjoy being trained while playing. What set them above the rest are their hunting skills which are natural to them.

Before you decide whether or not it might be the right pet for you and your family, you need to learn and invest a significant amount of time in getting to know what your pet really is. This chapter is an introduction of a Jack Russell Terrier. It includes basic facts and information, as well as the history of how it came about. This information, in combination with the succeeding information in the next chapters will help you decide if JRT's are the perfect dog companion for you.

Facts about Jack Russell Terrier

You might be wondering why this dog breed is named after a person. You may also be wondering who is Jack Russell. This breed is named after Reverend Jack Russell from England. This breed was originally made to frighten foxes with their barking. They were meant to be watch dogs, but they are not meant to kill the intruders.

Jack Russell Terriers are confused with other Terrier species like Parson Russell Terrier and Russell Terrier but they are all different from each other. What separates the

JRT from the two is that JRT's are smaller (than Parson) and larger (than Russell Terrier).

This breed is known to have a dominant attitude towards humans and other dogs. This makes them look very tough though they are not as big as the other dogs. The behavior that they exhibit is still because of their natural hunting instinct. It can be beneficial because this breed tends to be protective of their owners once they have established a relationship with their owners which makes training is very crucial to this breed.

When it comes to grooming, one of the most recognizable problems that a Jack Russell Terrier has is that their coat sheds too much. This means that owners should have time in brushing their coat once a day.

Jack Russell Terriers are very fun to play with because of their very athletic and energetic personality. Their playtime can be incorporated with training to make sure that they are exhibiting a good behavior towards people and other dogs.

Summary of Jack Russell Terrier Facts

Pedigree: Jack Russell Terrier Club of America

AKC Group: Terrier

Breed Size: Small

Height: 10-15 inches (25-38 cm) tall

Weight: weighs 6-8 kg

Coat Texture: may be smooth, broken, or rough

Color: white should be the dominant color with tan or black markings (from chestnut tan to the lightest shade of tan); can also appear as tricolor having consistent patches

Eyes: small almond eyes that is dark and expressive

Ears: button, drop ears should be falling forward

Tail: erect when moving and dropping when at rest; 4-5 inches in length

Temperament: can be easily trained, intelligent, brave, agile, active, obedient,

Strangers: sociable when trained well

Other Dogs: good with proper socialization but may have barking tendencies because of his hunting instincts

Other Pets: generally not good with other pets

Training: Highly trainable

Exercise Needs: requires a lot of exercise and play time with the use of lively activities; about 40 minutes a day

Health Conditions: generally healthy but may be prone to certain health conditions such as Cataracts, Glaucoma, Luxating Patella, Hereditary ataxia, Legg-Calve-Perthes Disease, Cerebral Ataxia, Congestive Heart Failure, Myasthenia Gravis, and Pituitary Dwarfism etc.

Lifespan: average 13-16 years or more

Jack Russell Terrier Breed History

What is very obvious in this breed is that it was named after a man named Russell. Jack Russel was from England who was the first man to breed a Jack Russell Terrier that is used for fox hunting. They used JRT's to flush away foxes. During that time, this breed was called a Fox Terrier. The terriers that Jack Russell has owned are white. He prefers this color so that the Terriers will be distinguished from the foxes.

In the year 1819, Jack Russell purchased a Terrier that he named "Trump". This terrier has patches around his tail, ears and eyes that has a tan color. This is how the breeding program got on board which produced dogs that formed a distinct breed. After sometime, this is where the modern Jack Russell Terrier came about.

Jack Russell Terriers are not recognized by the American Kennel Club but there is such a thing as a Jack Russell Terrier Club of America and many other countries have this breed as Kennel Club recognized.

Chapter Two: Jack Russell Terrier Requirements

Getting a dog is not just getting a breed that you've heard about, or what is popular, or what your neighbor has. There is such a thing as compatibility of a pet to its dog owner. Not every dog is the right dog for you. You have to make sure that it fits you, your family and the environment that you have.

This chapter contains information about the pros and cons of having a Jack Russell Terrier breed as a pet. It also discusses the average associated cost, and licensing which is required for you to become a legitimate JRT owner if you fix on to be one.

Do You Need a License?

There are certain regulations and restrictions that should be taken in to consideration when purchasing a dog, or in this case Jack Russell Terrier. Acquiring a license for your pets can be different depending on the country, state and region that you are in.

In the United States, there is no federal requirement for getting a license for your pets, but it is the State that regulars these kinds of rules. Though it is not required for you dogs to get a license, it is important that you do so. It will not just provide a protection for your pet, but also to you as a pet owner. An identification number is placed in your dog licensed which is directly linked to your contact details as the owner. This can be very helpful in case your pet gets lost.

It is important to take note that before you can get your dog a license, you must be vaccinated against rabies. This is the only requirement for you to acquire a license. Dog license are renewable every year which means that you have to get another rabies vaccination.

How Many JRT's should You Keep?

It is advisable to keep one Jack Russell Terrier per home. As mentioned in some sections of this chapter, JRT's requires a lot of time and attention when it comes to training. It will be hard for you to train a lot of JRT's. Also, this kind of breed is not an easy breed for first time dog owners. This breed is also has a heavy shedding coat which makes them high maintenance when it comes to grooming. This can also prove a point of owning one Jack Russell Terrier.

Owning more than one of any breed is still up to the pet owner since it takes a significant amount of effort in giving them all their needs. Of course, these needs do not only mean that you will provide for their physical daily needs, but also the significant time and affection that is vital for their growth and development. You must be willing to give your best effort in all the aspects of your life when you decide to get a dog.

Do JRT's get Along with Other Pets?

This breed was especially bred for hunting purposes which explains why they do not get a long much with other pets as compared to other breeds. JRT's tend to be aggressive and dominant that is why other pet may tend to feel intimidated around them. But through proper training and socialization, they can get along well eventually.

This breed does not only have natural hunting instincts, but they are also highly energetic. Their energy may have the tendency to shy away other dogs. This may also be a trigger for other pets to quarrel with the JRT.

How Much Does it Cost to Keep a JRT?

You may think getting a dog is just easy as 1, 2, 3! But of course, it entails a lot of responsibilities as a pet owner. Owning a pet does not come cheap because you need to provide for their needs to make sure that they grow up healthy and reach their life expectancy.

This section is an overview of the expenses of owning a Jack Russell Terrier. The expenses listed below include veterinary care, food and treats, toys, grooming and cleaning supplies. This can help you determine whether your pocket is ready for owning a pet.

Initial Costs

The average cost in purchasing a JRT from a reputable breeder is about $800 to $1,000. It is important to buy from a reputable breeder because it will save you money and effort from getting a dog that has a lot of health issues. Other initial cost to factor in includes crate, leash and color, initial vaccination/licensing, spay/neuter and grooming supplies. Prices may vary on different locations, but below is an average of each of the initial purchase cost:

Initial Costs Overview

Spaying or Neutering	$200
Medical Examination	$70
Crate	$50
Vaccination/Licensing	$75
Leash and Collar	$30
Grooming Supplies	$35
Total	$460

Having a pet is also like having a child. There is really a need for you to spend money to take good care and maintain your pet. If you do not take good care of your pet, you might find yourself losing them eventually. These expenses will surely add up to your everyday expenditure, but it will surely be worth it.

Remember that providing the dogs needs is also a way of showing your love and affection for them.

Monthly Costs

The monthly costs associated with keeping a Jack Russell Terrier can also be quite expensive. Some of the things that need to be bought on a monthly basis are food and treats, annual license renewal, toy replacements, and veterinary exams. Provided in this section is an overview of each of these costs as well as an estimate for each cost.

Food and Treats: total of $50 (£32.50)

Feeding your Jack Russell Terrier a healthy diet is very important for its health and wellness, especially for a very active and huge pet. A high-quality diet for dogs may not be cheap and highly depends on the brand. The right amount of nutrients should be provided to maintain its healthy and appealing physique. You should be prepared to spend around $40 for a high-quality dog food which will last you about a month. You should also include a monthly budget of at least $10 for treats, that way he/she can be rewarded every time he/she did a good job in training or behaving.

Grooming Costs: approximately $9 to $12.50 (£8 - £11.25)

You should plan to have your Jack Russell Terrier professionally groomed about twice a year (depends on how much your dog sheds) in order to keep his skin and coat in good health. You should budget about $10.50 (£8 - £11.25) per month.

License Renewal: average of $2.00 (£1.30)

The cost to license your Jack Russell Terrier is generally about $20 and you can renew the license for the same price each year, some states may cost more. License renewal cost divided over 12 months is about $2 per month.

Veterinary Exams: approximately $7.00 (£4.55)

In order to keep your Jack Russell Terrier healthy you should take him to the veterinarian at least twice a year; keep in mind that you may need to take him more often while he is a puppy to give him the vaccines he needs. The average cost for a vet visit is about $40 (£26) so, if you have two visits per year, it averages to about $7 (£4.55) per month.

Additional Costs: $15 (£9.75)

In addition to the cost for food, grooming, license renewal, and vet visits you will have to cover other costs on occasion. These costs may include replacements for toys, a larger collar as your puppy grows, cleaning products, and more. You won't have to cover these costs every month but you should include it in your budget to be safe.

An overview of these costs is provided for you in on the next section. Costs may vary depending on brand as well as location and the current exchange rate.

Monthly Expenses Overview

Needs	Monthly Costs
Food and Treats	$50 (£32.50)
Grooming Costs	$9 to $12.50 (£8 - £11.25)
License Renewal	$2 (£1.30)
Veterinary Exams	$7 (£4.55)
Other Costs	$15 (£9.75)
Total	$83 to $95.50 (£68.09 – £78.34)

Having a pet will greatly affect your spending that is why it is important to know if you are willing to adjust your budget. It is better to have an idea of what you should be expecting when it comes to owning a dog. Below is an average annual breakdown costs of owning one Jack Russell Terrier can be seen in the table:

Annual Costs	In USD	based on conversion rate of 1GBP=1.438 USD
Food expenses	Approximately $525	£365.21
Veterinarian Bills	Approximately $699	£486.25
Other costs (toys, treats and other accessories)	Approximately $545	£379.12
Grooming	Approximately $700	£486.78
Annual Vaccines, Heartworm preventative, and flea preventative	Approximately $800	£556.32
Total	$3,269	£2,273.68

What are the Pros and Cons of Jack Russell Terrier?

Before choosing a pet, it is important that you get to know them better first. Every dog is different, every breed is unique. That is the reason why it is important to get to know them first by doing some research. This can help you decided whether a certain breed is suitable for you. This section contains a list of pros and cons in having a Jack Russell Terrier. This can help you determine whether this breed fits you well.

Pros for Jack Russell Terrier

Get this type of breed…

- If you are not a first time dog owner and you have a lot of patience in training dogs
- If you can handle an energetic dog
- If you want a dependable watch dog, bit at the same time sociable around strangers
- If you want a medium-sized dog

Cons for the Jack Russell Terrier

- They are challenging to train at first

- They have a very dynamic temperament which makes them hard to handle if not properly trained
- They like digging holes and destroying things if they are not properly house trained.
- They constantly shed and can leave a lot of hair all over the place
- They can be aggressive towards other dogs and pets
- They bark excessively

Chapter Three: Purchasing a Jack Russell Terrier

    With all the information that you have read from the previous chapters, I am sure that you have decided whether to get a Jack Russell Terrier or not. And if you are deciding to get one, it is important to know where and how to acquire this kind of breed. As a pet owner, you should be aware where you will be getting your pet to ensure its health.

This chapter talks about where to get a healthy Jack Russell Terrier, finding a reputable breeder and list of breeders and websites. Information about getting a JRT from a Rescue Adoption is also included. Finally, included in this chapter are tips on how to dog-proof your home.

Finding a Reputable Jack Russell Breeder

Once you've decided that the Jack Russell Terrier is the right dog for you, your next step is to find one. Purchasing a Jack Russell Terrier might be as easy as stopping in to your local pet store since it is such a popular breed, but you should ask yourself whether this is really the best option. Many pet stores receive their puppies from puppy mills – organizations which breed dogs as quickly as they can, keeping the dogs in squalid conditions. As a result of irresponsible breeding practices, the puppies are often malnourished or suffering from health problems. The best way to make sure you get a Jack Russell Terrier puppy in good health is to do your research and to purchase one from a reputable Jack Russell Terrier breeder.

Tips in Choosing a Reputable Breeder

The difference between a reputable breeder and a puppy producer is that the former spends large amounts of time and money on the best interest of the breed, while the latter is often motivated by profit. However, in order to find a good Jack Russell Terrier breeder, you may have to do some research first. Once you've compiled a list of several Jack Russell Terrier breeders you then need to go through them to choose the best option. You don't want to run the risk of purchasing a puppy from a hobby breeder or from someone who doesn't follow responsible breeding practices. Keep in mind that when you purchase a Jack Russell Terrier puppy you are making a 15 year commitment!

Here are the following things you need to do to help you find a reputable Jack Russell Terrier breeder:

- Ask around at veterinary offices, groomers, and pet stores for referrals to Jack Russell Terrier breeders and assemble as much information as you can about each one.

- Visit the website for each breeder (if they have one) and check to see if the breeder is registered with a national or local breed club

- Contact each breeder individually and ask them questions about their knowledge of the Jack Russell Terrier breed as well as their breeding experience.

- Ask specific questions about the breeder's program and the dogs used to produce the puppies. Ask what the breeder does to prevent the passing of congenital conditions to the puppies.

- Remove the breeders from your list who do not seem to be knowledgeable about the breed or if they seem to be just hobby breeders looking to make a buck.

- Eliminate breeders from your list who refuse to answer your questions or who do not seem genuinely concerned for the wellbeing of their puppies.

- Schedule a visit with several breeders and ask for a tour of the facilities – check to make sure they are clean and that the dogs look healthy.

- Narrow down your list of breeders and make your selection – you should also ask about the breeder's preferences for putting down a deposit on a puppy.

- Place your deposit to reserve a puppy – in the next section you will receive tips for choosing a puppy from a litter.

Rescue Dogs Adoption

As an alternative to purchasing a Jack Russell Terrier puppy from a legitimate breeder, you should also consider adopting a rescue dog. Not only will you be doing your part in the war against puppy mills, but you will be providing a homeless dog with a loving home and new lease on life. There are many benefits associated with adopting a rescue dog and you might even be able to find a purebred Jack Russell Terrier puppy.

Adoption is much more affordable than purchasing a purebred puppy from a breeder and the dog is likely to have already been housebroken and may also have some amount of obedience training as well.

List of Breeders and Rescue Websites

In this section, you'll be given recommended websites on reputable breeders as well as rescue dogs associations in United States and United Kingdom, once you have narrow down your list of breeders, you can go and check to see the best option for you.

Jack Russell Terrier Breeders

Blue Creek

<www.bluecreekjackrussellterriers.com>

River Bottom

<www.roverbottomjackrussells.com>

British Grit

<www.BritishGrit.com>

Honey Tree

<www.HoneyTreeJRT.com>

Shavano Creek

<www.shavanocreek.com>

Conasauga

<www.conasaugajackrussellterriers.com>

Rock Chalk

<www.rockchalkterriers.com>

Diamond Gates

<www.DiamondGatesJRT.com>

Bojaxs

<www.bojaxsjrtmidmich.com>

Conquest

<www.conquestterriers.com>

High Range

<www.high-range.com>

James River

<JamesRiverJackRussellTerriers.com>

<u>Rescue Adoption</u>

Jack Russell Terrier Rescue of Colorado

<http://www.jrtrescueco.org>

AZ Jack Russell Rescue, Inc.

<http://jrto.wordpress.com/>

Jack Russell Rescue of Scottsdale

<http://www.jrtconnection.com/rescue.html>

Texas Russell Rescue

<http://www.russellrescue.com>

Russell Rescue Inc Oklahoma

<http://russellrescueok.petfinder.com>

Dogwood Rescue Society

<http://www.dogwoodrescue.org>

Tips on Purchasing a Jack Russell Terrier

Your chosen Jack Russell Terrier will be part of your family for an extended period so make sure to select the right dog for your family. Remember to not impulsively purchase that cute puppy in the window of your local pet shop to avoid many of the problems experienced by new puppy owners and save yourself a lot of heartaches. If you want to own a pet, escape from impulse buying.

It is recommended to purchase your Jack Russell Terrier puppy from a trusted and reputable, registered show Jack Russell Terrier breeder. It is very simple to select a dedicated breeder. Be sure also to avoid a registered backyard. Just ask if either the parent of the JRT is a champion and how many wins the breeder has bred. Also, ask the number of years the breeder has been showing their Jack Russell Terrier. This will give you the best opportunity of obtaining a companion who is a true representative of its breed. Never be fooled into purchasing a JRT from a registered backyard breeder. It is recommended that you must research the JRT breed thoroughly before buying.

The following are the questions you should ask the breeder before buying the JRT:

- Ask to see and visit the puppy and the parents in the breeder's home
- Ask to see both the parents because this will give you an idea of how the puppy will be as an adult. Do not buy a Jack Russell Terrier from a breeder that refuses to allow you to come to their place and see the parents of the JRT.
- If you are buying online, ask for more photos of the puppy at different angles to make sure it is not a scam. Also, ask to forward the photos of the parents to you.
- Ask questions about the size of the Jack Russell Terrier. A good breeder can tell you the puppies' current weight.
- Also, ask the breeder JRT will require.
- Ask about any health problems. Has the JRT been vet checked? Are they wormed on regular basis? Has the JRT been micro chipped?
- Ask if the parents of the puppy are DNA profiled.

- Ask if the breeder has been involved in Jack Russell Terrier rescue. Only purchase a puppy from a breeder who is dedicated to the breed.
- Ask if the breeder belongs to a Breed Club or Association. In the United States, puppies should be registered with the AKC (American Kennel Club). Take note, you must only purchase AKC registry puppies. This is because the AKC has strict rules of requirements and membership from the breeders. This rule is a good safeguard for a dog buyer.
- Ask if the breeder has a contract. A reputable breeder will have a contract that must spell out all conditions of sale.
- Ask if the breeder has a website. Most good breeders have a website. Also, be sure to avoid breeders who offer credit card or other easy payment methods online, including PayPal. Beware of the breeders who are in a hurry to sell their pet and close the deal.

If you are really interested in purchasing a Jack Russell Terrier dog, whether it is adult or puppy, do not hesitate to visit the Jack Russell Terrier Directory. It lists the very best Jack Russell Terrier breeders, AKC Registered JRT Breeders and Reputable Kennel Club.

Selecting a Healthy Jack Russell Terrier

A Jack Russell Terrier breed is very prone to certain canine health problems and diseases. I am not telling that your JRT will get these diseases but you must be aware that your dog is healthy so it will not be difficult to take care of them.

Keeping an eye for early signs of medical problems of your dog is of utmost importance; it could save you a lot of stress, time and money in the long run – not to mention your dog's health. This section will give you information if your Jack Russell Terrier dog is healthy to keep.

- **Monitor their eating habits**

If your dog ignores his drink or food for more than 24 hours, you must see a vet immediately, especially if your dog is usually a big eater.

- **Do a body check**

You should be doing a full body check of your dog on a weekly basis. You can gently run your hand over all the parts of your dog's body and check for cuts, lumps, inflammation and any signs of discomfort.

- **Observe on their walking**

Watch the way your dog moves when you're out on walks. Observe how he walks and runs. Does he ever seem stiff? Get easily tired? Or have a limp? Excessive panting and coughing may also indicate problems

- **Check their weight**

You should avoid obesity. This is the cause of a large number of problems in dogs. You should keep your dog on a steady, well-balanced diet. Seek advice sooner if things start to get out of control rather than later.

- **Monitor their toilet habits**

Constipation, diarrhea, blood and mucus are the four things to look out for in your stool of your dog. Also, if the urine is dark, blooded or cloudy, then you must already be sensitive on that. Keep an eye on their toilet habits and make sure it is regular. Be sure also that the appearance is consistent.

- **Check their mouth**

Check your dog's mouth for anything out of the ordinary. Gums must be pink. If you see darker/redder patches, it may indicate a problem. You must also check for growths and lumps, and make sure that the teeth are clear. Observe also their breath as unusually bad breath could be an indication of digestive problems.

- **Check their eyes**

    Eyes of dogs should be clear and the pupils should be of the same size. Check for ingrowing hair or eye lashes that look like it's causing a problem. Make sure also that there is no excessive discharge or signs of irritation. Visit a vet if there is.

- **Check their nose**

    The nose of dogs should be cool and moist. Keep an eye out for excessive sneezing, discharge and make sure that breathing is unobstructed and easy.

- **Check their feet**

    Scrutinize your dog's feet for any grazes, cuts or growths. Long nails may cause problems and should be trimmed, either with file or dog clippers. You have to be careful when cutting the nails of your dogs to avoid bleeding.

- **Check their ears**

Lastly, check the ears of your dogs for wax build-up, bad odor, and swelling. Wax can be easily removed if done properly. Use cotton wool but you should never poke anything directly down your dog's ears.

This basic checklist should be properly observed and performed on a regular basis. Doing so will ensure that you catch any sign of trouble as early as possible. Always remember that if anything looks different on your Jack Russell Terrier, never hesitate to consult your vet.

Chapter Four: Caring Guidelines for Jack Russell Terrier

It is important that when you get a pet, you must have the willingness to care for it at all cost. The Jack Russell Terrier breed is not as hard to take care. Though you need a lot of patience to tame and train them, they can still be taught. Properly caring for your pets will result in to them having a good and long life. That is why it is important that as pet owners, you are willing to take all these tasks at hand because this will not just benefit your pet, but you as a pet owner as well.

This chapter includes basic information about how give your Jack Russell Terrier a healthy and a happy home and also how to set up his personal space in his crate. Tips about giving him the proper exercise is also found in this chapter.

Socializing Your Dog

The best time to socialize your JRT is when they are, in fact, a pup. Dogs are at their most receptive and sensitive between three and twelve weeks of age. The earlier you can get your dog socialized, the better. After those span of twelve weeks, it can be very difficult to get a puppy to accept anything unfamiliar.

- **Walk your dog daily** – introduce them to other dogs
  Dog walks have a great advantage in meeting new dogs and people as well as practice their proper behavior when they are out because you're just bound to run into more social situations when your dog is out for a walk than when staying at home.

- **Use a muzzle when other dogs come over**

    If you already know that your JRT barks or growls at other dogs, it can help if you let them use a muzzle. This prevents the danger of attacking or biting and it can also make the dogs calmer so they'll be more sensitive to meeting other dogs and have a more positive experience.

- **Expose your dogs to different social activities**

    If you can introduce your dog to a new activity once a week, it will go a long way in helping them socialize, be calm and more behaved.

Training Your Jack Russell Terrier Dogs

The good thing about Jack Russell Terriers is that they are very good with training; whether it is for heeling, housebreaking or performing tricks.

Training is a combined effort between the owner and the dog. The owner will take the important role of a teacher, while your JRT will be the great student. Jack Russell Terriers are pretty fast learners but it may take longer based on some other factors.

Two of the most important things to be considered will be how strictly you will be to stick with the training and how many learning opportunities your JRT have.

A lot of these things depend on you, as an owner. It will be important for you to understand and follow the housebreaking guidelines and a big part of this will be how often times your dog has a chance to train his lessons.

Potty training

A lot of owners believe that toy breed dogs can easily be trained to use a litter box or pee pads. This is not as easy as it sounds, but it is still possible. JRTs may have a hard time using pee pads because they have a natural instinct to want to choose on the right spot to pee or poop.

However, indoor training can be easily done if you are persistent and if you have a cooperative, JRT.

There should be a chosen spot as the 'designated bathroom area' and this will be the term used whether you have pee pads in a corner that is already set up or have an indoor grass mat for your JRT.

Preparing to Housebreak Your Jack Russell Terrier

- **Choose the designated area**

Take note that you should never allow your JRT to go outside somewhere. There should be one certain area to be chosen as designated bathroom area. Ideally, it will be an area that ranges from 8 to 10 foot in diameter.

- **Choose a containment method**

A JRT that is not fully housebroken should never be free in either a room or the house especially if he is not well supervised.

- **Choose your reward treats**

A JRT is going to be more motivated to focus, be able to soak in the training, understand that he did something right, and look forward to the next training lesson if he is properly rewarded with treats.

- **Be ready for a speedy exit**

To have your JRT wearing his collar and to keep the leash right by the door is the final step in preparing to facilitate a fast exit to the designated area. It is highly recommended to have a harness. If you are not used to having one, you may at first think that they are difficult to take on and off.

You are already ready to housebreak your JRT successfully once you.

- Have chosen the best location for your dog's designated bathroom area that will be relatively easy to reach.

- Have set up a playpen or some other containment method for your dog to be at any time you can't keep an eye on him
- Have special training treats right by the exit door and have your dog's harness on him and his leash that is ready to spring into action

Housebreaking Tips

- Keep your JRT with you, as often as possible. If he will pee or poo, clap your hand loudly or call out his name to cause him to pause.
- Your prep should allow you to exit with your dog quickly, but carry him if needed.
- As your JRT is doing the deed, repeat a chosen word or phrase so that he can associate it with his actions. Some owners use 'bathroom' or 'piddy potty'.
- Bring your JRT outside with a specific schedule. If you are heading to the yard to get some exercise, bring him to his bathroom area first.
- Allow your JRT at least 15 minutes to find the perfect spot within the area, and for his bladder and bowel muscles to relax.
- If your JRT is done peeing, offer the reward treat right away. Always give praise to them at the same time.
- If there are in some cases that accidents happen in the house, it is important to clean the area with an

enzyme cleanser. This is because it might be announced to your JRT that 'This is the bathroom area'

Behavioral Problems

Active, intelligent, and a relatively healthy breed, Jack Russell Terriers make a great companion and also do well in competitions, including obedience and agility trials. Some JRTs may be prone to specific behavioral problems, so potential owners should consider the temperament of these dogs before adopting one.

Aggression and Fear

JRTs tend to be suspicious around strangers and they become intimidated to large people and animals because of their small size. Fear can turn to aggression and you should not consider your dog's fear as an endearing behavior.

Possessiveness and Territoriality

Jack Russell Terriers are likely to be possessive of toys and food because they have a strong reputation for being demanding to owners. You should train them by putting your hand in their bowl and playing toy exchange games when she is a puppy. This will decrease the likelihood of territorial behavior in adulthood

Excessive barking

JRTs are notoriously yappy dogs, especially when they are not socialized to strangers and loud noises. You can put your dog in a crate when they bark excessively loud and reward them for being calm and quiet when there are visitors.

Grooming Jack Russell Terrier Dogs

In regards to grooming, Jack Russell Terriers are on the higher level of maintenance. If grooming is not performed properly or on a regular basis, things can go out of control. The coat can become matted. Fur may become brittle. The skin may dry out. Tear stains might become excessive. Paws and nose might peel. In short, it can become a disaster.

Regular Jack Russell Terrier Grooming Tips

- **Toenails**

Make sure to clip your JRT's toenails with dog toenail clippers once every six or eight weeks. It will keep your dog's paws clean and healthy and will prevent him from scratching upon jumping up. Be sure not to cut their nails too close as this may hurt them.

- **Teeth**

You have to thoroughly brush your Jack Russell Terrier's teeth on a regular basis as this type of breed is prone to dental cavities. You have to use special toothpaste that contains enzymes to inhibit bacterial growth in the mouth.

- **Eyes**

Jack Russell Terriers tend to have a lot of discharge from their eyes that may cause an infection due to bacteria. Hence, it is important to clean the eye area of your JRT.

- **Trimming**

Your Jack Russell Terrier does not need to be shaved down during hot weather. There is no reason to shave your JRT's beautiful coat just because the weather is hot. It is because if the inner layer is shaved, it may never grow back again to once it was before. Little touch-ups to keep things clean and neat can be done every 2 to 3 months as needed.

Show Dog Jack Russell Terrier Training

You can go far beyond basic commands in training Jack Russell Terrier if you are committed and if you really wanted it to. JRTs are very well known for their exceptional learning skills. This makes them an ideal breed for the show ring.

The following information will give you an idea on how to use the right Jack Russell Terrier training to prepare your JRT to become a show dog.

- You need to understand the first aspect of training for a show is that it requires a lot of hard work. Unlike teaching your JRT basic commands, the lessons need to be taught are activities training.
- You should learn how to properly groom your JRT for a show. You can get it from a professional book, from a video or from a groomer itself.

You should make grooming an enjoyable experience just like Jack Russell Terrier training. It helps to get your JRT used to grooming because this will help him become more accustomed to being handled.

- Practice posing or stacking your dog as soon as he is comfortable with the grooming table. First, have him stay in his position for a few seconds. And then increase the time you make him stay on the table. Be sure to give him a lot of rewards for standing poised for a long period of time.

Once your dog knows how to stay poised, you can move to the next step of his training which is the inspecting your JRT as a judge will. You have to check his legs, teeth, feet, etc.

- You can enroll your JRT in handling classes
- Your dog will need leash training. This form of training is about putting him on a leash and then eventually allowing him to go wherever he wants.

Once your JRT is already familiar with changing directions, the next thing is to teach him on a loose head. Your dog will be taught to stand beside you when you stop, and then your dog will walk beside you, right or left side.

- You can also attend conformation training classes. These are to mirror show conditions, which make them an ideal place for show training. These classes will surely help you learn and fine tune all the skills that are required in a show ring.

Finally, before deciding to enter your JRT in a dog show, you should first attend a few shows so you can have an idea. The more you and your dog are prepared for a show, the more your training will pay off.

Chapter Five: Nutritional Needs of Jack Russell Terrier Dogs

The right way of feeding your Jack Russell Terrier is very essential in his overall health. How, how much, and how often are vital questions that needs to be answered in terms of feeding your JRTs. Jack Russell Terrier puppies need the right amount of nutrition to grow, adults need the best diet to maintain health and senior JRTs need the right food possible to meet the needs of an older dog.

This section will elaborate all the tips on how to feed your JRTs and the basic nutritional needs that they require in order to have a healthy immune system.

Tips for Feeding Your Jack Russell Terriers

Different foods have different amounts of calories so the recommended serving size will also vary. The right amount of food that a Jack Russell Terrier requires will vary on his age, activity level, and individual metabolism.

A good guideline about feeding the right amount of food is this. Recommended servings for puppies are 55 calories per pound while for adult JRTs are 45 calories per pound.

When your JRT is undergoing a growth spurt, his appetite may increase and if he appears to want more after finishing his meal, do not hesitate to offer a second serving. It is very impossible for a growing JRT puppy to eat too much.

Protein

Jack Russell Terriers have a tiny stomach and they cannot properly digest foods with a lot of filler especially that most dog food companies use grain and plant matter as filler in their foods. JRTs that do not get enough proteins may become malnourished and underweight. If you choose to buy commercial canned food, it should contain little to no filler. You can let your dog eat small amounts of boiled chicken or liver but be sure that it is cooked, as puppies' stomachs are not developed enough to digest raw food.

Dry Food

Tooth loss is very common for Jack Russell Terriers so in order to prevent it, you need to provide dry dog food which will keep your dog's teeth and gums healthy. Dry dog food to be chosen should be in small pieces so that it will be easy for tiny mouths to chew.

Treats

You cannot easily give your Jack Russell Terriers too many treats as a tiny dog has a tiny stomach. Always remember that Jack Russell Terriers should never get people food. You can give your JRTs commercial treats for as long as there is no filler. This can serve as occasional treats or for positive reinforcement in training

Types of Commercial Dog Foods

Now let's discuss the three main types of commercial dog foods, which are wet, soft/moist, and dry. They are different in many aspects including moisture content, palatability, cost, and nutritional benefit.

- **Wet food**

Wet foods are usually sold in cans and contain 75 to 80 % water, 8-15% protein and 2-15% fat. Dogs eat more of this type of food without gaining weight because of the high moisture content. Canned foods, if compared to dry and soft/moist products offer the highest palatability, but wet food also has the highest cost per serving,

- **Dry Food**

Dry foods are packed in bags and contain 18-40% protein, 7-22% fat, 12-50% carbohydrates and about 10% moisture. It comes in different sizes, shapes, and colors because dog discerns the density, texture, shape and size of the food, and the way food may feel in the mouth contributes to palatability.

- **Soft or Moist Food**

This is usually sold in boxes and contains single-serving pouches. It contains approximately 15-25% protein, 5-10% fat, 25-35% carbohydrates, and approximately 30% water. This type of food is highly palatable and very convenient to serve and store.

How Often to Feed Jack Russell Terrier

The number of meals that you give to a JRT depends on his age. Feeding your dog the right amount of food can also be tricky. Below, you will know how much to feed your JRT depending on his age.

- **Brand new puppies**

It is recommended to free-feed during the first month of your JRT, meaning, fresh food is left out at all times. This is because blood sugar can drop quickly for young puppies, and one cause of this is not eating enough amount of food.

- **Puppies 3 months to 12 years**

In this age range, you must feed your Jack Russell Terrier puppy three times a day. You may consider buying a treat dispensing toy so that if you will be gone during the day for the mid-meal, your JRT will not miss his food.

- **JRTs 1 year and older**

      Some adult Jack Russell Terriers are good with eating three times a day, while some may be happy with two meals a day. Always take note that snacks should be given in addition to these feedings. Mostly, these are reserved for rewarding and training purposes.

Tips in Selecting a High-Quality Dog Food Brand

      As a pet owner, feeding your JRT a high-quality well-balanced food is one of the best things that you can do to keep your pet healthy. Picking the right food will keep your dog's hair coat sleek and shiny. It will also help strengthen his immune system and it will keep his digestive system in good health.

      In order to improve your JRT's diet, start by simply ignoring the labeling claims on commercial pet food. Look instead for AAFCO certification so that you can be sure it meets the basic requirements for vitamins and trace minerals.

What to look for in a dry pet food

      The first thing to look in dry pet food is meat. Dogs are carnivores and they thrive on a diet that is based on meat. Dogs do not need a lot of carbohydrates. The reason why grains and carbs are added to pet food is because they are way cheaper than meat, and they hold the kibbled bits together. They didn't add that for the sake of good nutrition for your meat-eating pet.

The quality and source of protein content in the formula are very important for your pet's health. The first thing to look for in a dog's food is the ingredient list like beef, turkey, lamb or chicken. Avoid any formula that makes use of unidentified sources, described non-specifically as meat, animal, or poultry.

How to Feed Your Jack Russell Terrier Dogs

Owning a JRT means understanding their feeding requirements. You should be knowledgeable about this because this is very important for their health. At any stages of their lives, they should be given a proper diet for their well-being and healthy growth.

If you are feeding your Jack Russell Terrier in a wrong way, it may result in some health problems. They may suffer from obesity or other diseases like strained ligaments and joints if you feed them too much. Take note that a puppy Jack Russell Terrier burns more calories quickly compared to adults. Therefore, it is very vital to understand the food requirement of your Jack Russell Terrier depending on his age.

Importance of quality food for your JRTs

Cheap dog foods contain various harmful ingredients which may affect the health of your JRT in a negative way. You have to be aware that various harmful by products and fillers are present in different dog foods and these have almost zero nutrition. It is good if you can feed your JRTs raw food diet.

The amount of food given to a JRT varies on the age, size, metabolism and the level of the activity of your dog. Recommended daily amount of food to a Jack Russell Terrier adult is ¼ to ½ cup of high quality dry food and these are given in two meals.

Below are the recommended servings for puppies:

- ½ cup of food for 1 pound puppy
- 1 cup of food for 3 pounds puppy
- 25 cups of food for 5 pound puppy
- 2 cups of food for 6 pounds puppy

There are changes according to requirements of the diet of pregnant, senior, and inactive Jack Russell Terriers so it is recommended consulting with the vet. Jack Russell Terriers burn more calorie compared to other breeds of dogs because they have high energy levels and require food at regular intervals. A growing JRT should be fed three to four times a day at regular intervals. When they reach adulthood, they should be fed the same amount of food twice a day.

Toxic Foods to Avoid

There are some foods that you should not feed your JRTs under any occasion. The list of foods below should be carefully avoided to keep your dog away from accidents.

- **Alcohol**

Alcoholic beverages or food products that contain alcohol may cause diarrhea, vomiting, central nervous system depression, decreased coordination, difficulty breathing, abnormal blood acidity, tremors, coma, and even death.

- **Avocado**

Dogs that might get a chance to eat avocado may cause cardiovascular damage or even death.

- **Chocolate, coffee, and caffeine**

All of these products contain substances called methylxanthines which can be found in cacao seeds. If these are ingested by dogs, they might experience diarrhea, vomiting, panting, excessive thirst and urination, abnormal heart rhythm, seizures and even death.

- **Citrus**

This can cause irritation and possibly even central nervous system depression if eaten in significant amounts.

- **Coconut and coconut oil**

This may not cause serious harm to your pet if ingested in just small amounts. But it may cause stomach upsets, loose stools or diarrhea.

- **Grapes and raisins**

These fruits can cause kidney failure although it is still not known what substance is present in grapes and raisins. Until more information is known about its toxic substance, it is still best to avoid feeding raisins and grapes to your dogs.

- **Macadamia nuts**

This can cause weakness, vomiting, depression, tremors and hyperthermia on dogs.

- **Milk and dairy**

Milk and other dairy products can cause dogs' diarrhea or other digestive problems.

- **Nuts**

Nuts contain a high amount of oils and fats that can cause vomiting and diarrhea and also pancreatitis in pets.

- **Onions, garlic, chives**

These herbs and vegetables can cause gastrointestinal irritation that could lead to red blood cell damage.

- **Raw/Undercooked Meat, Eggs, and Bones**

Raw eggs and meats may contain bacteria like Salmonella and E. coli that can be harmful not only to dogs but also to humans. On the other hand, raw bones can be very dangerous for a domestic pet that might choke on bones.

- **Salt and salty snack foods**

These can produce excessive thirst and urination, or even sodium ion poisoning for your JRTs which will lead to vomiting, diarrhea, tremors, depression, elevated body temperature, seizures and even death.

- **Xylitol**

This is used as a sweetener which can cause insulin release in most dogs, which can lead to liver failure.

- **Yeast dough**

This can cause gas to accumulate in your dog's digestive system that may lead to stomach bloat, and potentially twist that may become a life threatening emergency.

Chapter Six: Maintenance for Jack Russell Terrier Dogs

Let's assume that you already have your own Jack Russell Terrier dog. The most difficult part of owning one is the responsibility that comes with it. It is necessary to provide them their basic needs and keep them healthy all the time. In this section, you will be informed about how to properly take care of your dog and how to maintain their healthy lifestyle as well as their well-being.

Tips on How to Dog-Proof Your Home

If you already purchased your JRT, you should keep in mind that you have to provide a safe environment for them. There are steps to be taken to prepare your yard and home for your dog in order to eliminate any dangers. Baby proofing your home is similar to preparing your home for a new puppy. New dogs are impertinent by nature, so they would want to investigate everything even if those things could be dangerous. Therefore, you should make sure that each room of your home is a safe environment for your pet.

- **Dog proofing bathrooms and kitchens**

Bathrooms and kitchens could be dangerous for your pets because of the cleaning supplies, medications, and other chemicals. These are the two basic rooms in your home where dog proofing is imperative. Consider the following to keep your pets safe in the bathrooms and kitchens.

- Make sure to put items like cleaning supplies, laundry soaps and medications on high shelves.
- Keep all the food out of reach from your dogs because it might be dangerous for consumption. Even if the

food does not cause a threat, the packaging could be the problem.

- Always keep trash cans covered so that your dog won't get into the garbage
- Some pets are not only curious but quite clever so consider installing childproof latches on cabinets.
- Avoid your pet from jumping into the dryer before turning it on.
- Block any small spaces such as small spaces behind the washer and dryer or holes in cabinets.
- Always keep the toilet lid down so that your pet can not drink harmful chemicals.

- **Dog proofing the living room**

Not only the kitchen and the bathroom pose most serious threats for pets but also the living room also because it contains items that could also be dangerous. In order to make sure that your pets are safe in the living room, you must consider the following:

- Move your plants out of reach from your JRTs and better yet, assure that all plants in your home or yard is safe for your pet and is not poisonous to them.
- Make sure that any heating or air vents have proper covers

- Keep dangling wires from stereos, televisions, lamps and other items out of reach of your JRTs
- Put away from your dogs any breakable items such as knick knacks that your JRT can knock over and break
- Put away any toys or kid games that have small pieces because this can be a choking hazard to your curious JRT.

- **Dog proof the bedroom**

The bedroom might be safe for your JRTs and not a lot are needed to be done here to dog proof. However, there are still few steps that can be taken to make your bedroom safer for your JRTs:

- Keep any medicine, lotion or cosmetics that are placed on a bedside table, out of reach.
- Make sure that your JRTs can not access and chew any electric wires in some areas.
- Keep laundry and shoes out of reach of your JRTs because buttons and strings can pose a choking hazard and potentially even more serious issues if ingested
- Make sure that your JRTs are not staying or sleeping in drawers or closets before shutting them

- **Dog proof the garage and backyard**

The backyard and the garage can be home to a number of items that are risky for your JRTs just as with the kitchen and bathroom. If you are thinking of leaving your JRTs in the garage and backyard, you must first consider the following:

- Make sure to clean the floor of the garage so that chemicals like antifreeze are nowhere to be found. Your JRT can die if these chemicals are ingested.
- Move all chemicals in the garage to high shelves or in a closet that can't be accessed by your pets.
- Check the fence for any spaces or holes where your JRT might squeeze through and patch them up or consider boarding the spaces.

Habitat Requirements for Jack Russell Terrier Dogs

The great thing about Jack Russell Terriers is that they don't take up too much space to roam around with, but aside from space, the main thing your Jack Russell Terrier needs in terms of its habitat is lots of love and affection from his human companions and adequate daily exercise. Even though the Jack Russell Terrier is sometimes too stubborn and cutely witty, it is a very loyal and affectionate breed that bonds closely with family, so you should make an effort to spend some quality time with your Jack Russell Terrier each and every day. If you're Jack Russell Terrier doesn't get enough attention he may be more likely to develop problem behaviors like chewing or excessive barking and potential aggression as well as separation anxiety.

In addition to playing with your Jack Russell Terrier and spending time with him every day, you also need to make sure that his needs for exercise are met. The Jack Russell Terrier doesn't require extensive exercises but it is still recommended to take your dog for a walk or run once in a while plus some active play time, this is very important for your Jack Russell Terrier. You should also make sure your Jack Russell Terrier gets plenty of mental stimulation from interactive toys and games.

Toys and Accessories for Jack Russell Terrier Dogs

JRT's supplies will change as each young puppy matures into an adult dog and then yet again when then also when they become a senior. The products associated with Jack Russell Terrier clearly indicate if they're appropriate for their age. When you are already ready to welcome your new JRT into your home, make sure you already have their personal supplies stocked to help keep them happy and healthy at every stage of their lives.

With the right nutrients and ingredients, JRT's food supplies can help give your Jack Russell Terriers the building blocks they need to prolong their years of face licking and tail wagging. You can also provide your JRTs treats to keep them feeling rewarded, focused and excited to learn new tricks and right manners.

However, if your JRTs aren't pleased by treats, you can give them a collection of dog toys for every preference. In that way, you can have a reward system for your JRT or simply just give them some much needed exercise with their plush dog ball or toys.

In addition to treating and toy fueled playtime, daily walks with your JRTs' accessories can provide great bonding moments. There is a large array of JRT's accessories and clothes for every occasion and season to keep them looking comfortably stylish wherever they go.

If your JRTs are new to walks, there are also specialized dog accessories that are already available to help leash train your JRTs, so you can make sure your young JRT can respect the rules of the road as they explore the world outside of their homes. There are also dog training supplies available in the market to reinforce good behavior like pee pads, clickers, and bark collars.

Additionally, your JRT deserves the best bed or crating dog supplies for their size and sleeping style. Dog crate covers, heated bed products, and blankets can also make for a more comfortable good night's rest.

For your on-the-go needs of your JRTs, there are also dog carriers and car seat accessories available in the market if you want to make trips to the park. Getting the right car accessories for your JRTs doesn't just only make you hassle-free during travel, but they will also make it more comfortable and safer too.

Also, if your vet prescribes or recommends something for your pup, you must really invest on it like dog products to tackle fleas, ticks, and more.

Tips for Keeping Your Dogs Happy Indoors and Outdoors

Jack Russell Terriers are indoor dogs so they must always be kept inside our homes, in a safely fenced yard, or on-leash. But they are not inside our homes all the time. They can still go for a walk at the dog park provided they have a full supervision. This section will enumerate the tips that will help your dog stay happy whether indoors or outdoors.

Jack Russell Terriers like to see what's going on outside so why not open the curtains of your homes so they can have a foresight on the outside. Most dogs enjoy a nice view, especially when it's sunny outside, the incoming light can improve your dog's mood. Open also the windows so that your JRTs can get some fresh air. But make sure to do this only if you are at home and there's someone to look after your JRT. Puzzle games are also great for a dog while they are indoors. It can be a nice pass time and can stimulate your dog's brain especially that you are not always there to play with them.

You can also try buying a treadmill for your JRTs. It can be a great way to keep your JRTs in good shape when you have no time to exercise them. Your dog then can definitely exercise at home when it's convenient whether you are sick or the weather is bad. Having a bond with your dog indoors is the best thing to do when you can't go outside for a walk. Make sure to always make time for your JRTs. You may snuggle on the couch, make a brushing session, or even a massage will definitely keep them happy. You can also practice training your dog when you are inside your homes. Although it may seem boring, your JRT might enjoy this because it gives them a job and they are getting to work with you. Taking even just a small amount of time to practice tricks, obedience, etc. will keep your dog's mind sharp and will eliminate boredom.

As mentioned earlier, Jack Russell Terrier dogs are intended in indoors so it is not really recommended that he should be treated as an outdoor dog, even though he can moderately tolerate the hot and cold weather. So it's better off leaving him inside your home with your family.

You can let your JRTs go outdoors like in the yard when he already reached eight weeks old. However, make sure that there are no other dogs that can get in and this includes other dogs you own. Make sure also that your yard is clean and that you have treated the ground for weeds and fleas. When your JRTs reached eight weeks old, you can take them outside for as long as you hold him at all times. His feet can never touch the ground outside until he has had all the necessary shots except in your back yard if it is safe.

You must avoid taking your JRTs out in public areas until his puppy shots are already completed. This includes walking along the footpath, being out in your front yard, at the shops, in parks, in yards belonging to neighbours and so on. Your JRTs must be 12-16 weeks old before he can be safely taken outdoors but be sure you still have his leash at all times.

It's very unhealthy to keep your dog indoors at all times. Your home won't have sufficient space for him to roam around unless you have a spacious mansion. It is necessary to give your JRTs a small amount of sunshine each day for Vitamin D. Besides, getting enough exercise for your JRTs is very essential. You have to plan your walks the same time each day so that he has something to look forward to. Exercises are important because it helps him get off diseases and he could be able to smell, hear and see new things. This makes his hearth healthy and balances out his muscle tone.

Chapter Seven: Showing Your Jack Russell Terrier

The Jack Russell Terrier is a wonderful dog to keep as a pet but this breed has the potential to be so much more than that. These dogs are very clever, active and trainable which makes them a great choice as a show dog.

In order to show your Jack Russell Terrier, however, you have to make sure that he meets the requirements for the breed standard and you need to learn the basics about showing dogs.

In this chapter you will receive information about the breed standard for Jack Russell Terrier breeds and you will find general information about preparing your dog for show.

Jack Russell Terrier Breed Standard

The Jack Russell Terrier is an alert and enthusiastic breed that is accepted and recognized by the American Kennel Club (AKC). This section will give you the breed standard and general guidelines on how to present your dog.

Official Jack Russell Terrier Standard

General Appearance: very active, intelligent, strong, medium body length, keen expression, flexible, smart and elegant movements, having a coat that may be smooth, broken or rough

Height: 25-38 cm or 10-15 inches

Temperament: readily trainable, intelligent, bold, fearless, confident, friendly

Head: Skull is flat, with a moderate width and decreasing of length to the eye, having strong jaws and has a well-defined stop (tee shaped head, long wedge, apple head)

Ears: good texture and great mobility, button ear. Should always fall forward towards the ground

Eyes: intense expression of eye, almond shaped, pigmented eyelid

Gait: having a free and well-coordinated movement

Mouth: powerful jaws, pigmented lips that are firm having well-built teeth with a scissor bite

Neck: length should be 2/3 of the length of the back

Forequarters: must be well laid back and sloping evidently cut at the withers; should be straight boned with the joints having correct alignment and it should be strong and having elbows upright to the body

Hindquarters: having a good angle, muscular and strong which enables them to have a good impetus, hooks must be straight from behind

Body: having a narrow, shallow chest having an athletic disposition; legs should not be too distant, having average sized hands, having a straight back

Tail: Must be proportioned to the length of the body, set high and an average of 4 inches in length

Coat Quality: coat should be smooth, rough or broken. No undergrowth and not too wooly

Coat Colors: White must prevail but brown, black, and tan markings are acceptable

Tips on Preparing Your Jack Russell Terrier for Show

Once you've determined that your Jack Russell Terrier achieved all the requirements of the breed standard, and then you can think about entering him in a dog show. Dog shows occur all year-round in many different locations so check the AKC or Kennel Club website for shows in your area. Remember, the rules for each show will be different so make sure to do your research so that you and your Jack Russell Terrier are properly prepared for the show.

Here are some things you need to keep in mind while prepping your dog for show:

- Make sure that your Jack Russell Terrier has been housetrained completely before registering him for a show.

- Ensure that your dog is properly socialized to be in an environment with many other dogs and people.

- Make sure that your Jack Russell Terrier has had at least basic obedience training. He needs to respond to your commands and follow your lead in the show ring.

- Research the requirements for the individual show and make sure your Jack Russell Terrier meets them before you register.

- Take your Jack Russell Terrier to the vet to ensure that he is healthy enough for show and that he is caught up on his vaccinations – the bordatella vaccine is especially important since he'll be around a lot of other dogs.

- Pack a bag of supplies for things that you and your Jack Russell Terrier are likely to need at the show.

- Have your Jack Russell Terrier groomed the week of the show and take steps to make sure his coat stays in good condition.

Quick Checklist

Here are some things that may come in handy before, during and after the show:

- Registration information
- Dog crate or exercise pen
- Grooming table and grooming supplies
- Food and treats
- Food and water bowls
- Trash bags
- Medication (if needed)
- Change of clothes
- Food/water for self
- Paper towels or rags
- Toys for the dog

Chapter Eight: Breeding Your Jack Russell Terrier Dogs

Are you prepared in breeding your Jack Russell Terrier dog? One must be fully prepared before breeding. Do you have enough money to do this? This is because breeding involves many veterinarian bills. Do you have time? Newborn puppies need to have a careful eye on them around the clock. Do you have the emotional strength?

Even the best breeders experience loss. Read on if you really want to become a breeder but take note that there are a lot of things that you should know. This chapter will give you an idea of breeding one.

Basic Dog Breeding Information

The first rule that to you have to understand and follow is that breeding is best left to professional breeders. But of course, it is also essential that you know the basics of breeding a dog. A lot of things are involved, and it is important that you know your responsibilities and all the things that you need to observe to ensure that the breeding will produce healthy JRT puppies.

There is somewhat a high level of loss in puppies. This is caused by different kinds of reasons, and can also happen in any breed not only on JRTs, but this happens more often in toy breeds. Anyone who is breeding must understand and accept that puppies may die inexplicably at times. It is heartbreaking and tragic of course.

Mating Behavior of dogs

When a female dog or what they termed it as the 'bitch' is in heat, there are a few signs that can point towards her beginning this process. These are:

- Being nervous
- Easily spooked
- Easily distracted
- Urinating more than usual

Her personality may also alter due to the abrupt change in her hormones. Male dogs are ready to breed from the age of 18 months to 4/5 years old according to breeding dogs Info center. An interesting fact about male dogs is that when they hit the age around 10 years old, the semen they produce will not be capable of impregnating a female.

Ovulation Timing

A lot of breeders today use lab tests to measure Progesterone, vaginal cytology, and luteinizing hormone to determine when ovulation occurs. Breeders know that the cycle is usually 21 days despite what some male dogs think. What may be normal for one dog may differ from another. Some bitches' cycle on schedule, while others mate and ovulate from 12-21 days. Some have 'clear heats', false or flaky seasons, or even false pregnancies. Here are the average estrus changes an owner may expect in normal heat cycles.

- **Day 1:** Attention to rear and licking. Discharge is bright or dark red color, swelling of the vulva. You can start counting heat cycle from when the blood hits the ground.

- **Day 2 – 7:** Bright red discharge with swelling increases

- **Day 8 – 10:** The color begins to lighten and turn into pinkish. Swelling is at peak and the vulva has a spongy feel and look.

- **Day 9 – 14:** The color changes from light pink to clear or straw colored. The swelling is down and the vulva may appear hard or dry on edges.

- **Day 14 – 21:** Color clears, discharge and swelling is almost gone and bitch may already act receptive, but is still snappy. You can count 58-62 days for puppies! But there also exceptions to the rule. Some bitched may mate and conceive as late as 22 days.

Tips for Breeding Your Jack Russell Terrier

Now that you know the basics about breeding dogs you can learn the specifics about Jack Russell Terrier. The Jack Russell Terrier has a gestation period lasting about 58 - 68 days (or about 9 to 10 weeks). The gestation period is the period of time following conception during which the puppies develop in the mother's uterus. The average litter size for the Jack Russell Terrier breed is between 4 to 8 puppies. Keep in mind that new mothers will often have smaller litters – the next few litters will generally be larger before the litter size starts to taper off again.

To increase your chances of a successful breeding, you need to keep track of your Jack Russell Terrier's estrus cycle. Once your female reaches the point of ovulation, you can introduce her to the male dog and let nature take its course. Breeding behavior varies slightly from one breed to another, but you can expect the male dog to mount the female from behind (as long as she is receptive). If the breeding is successful, conception will occur and the gestation period will begin.

While the puppies are developing inside your female Jack Russell Terrier's uterus, you need to take special care to make sure the female is properly nourished. You do not need to make changes to your dog's diet until the fourth or fifth week of pregnancy. At that point you should slightly increase her daily rations in an amount proportionate to her weight gain. It is generally best to offer your dog free feeding because she will know how much she needs to eat. Make sure your dog's diet is high in protein as well as calories and fat to support the development of her puppies – calcium is also very important.

Signs that your dog is pregnant:

- Fast nipple growth or appearance
- Less energetic
- More affectionate or clingy
- Experiences mood swings
- The stomach will expand and get firm
- The dog will clean herself more than the usual
- May attempt to build a dog's nest.

Labor Process of Jack Russell Terrier

By the eighth week of pregnancy you should start preparing yourself and your dog for the whelping. This is the time when you should set up a whelping box where your female dog can comfortably give birth to her puppies. Place the box in a quiet, dim area and line it with newspapers and old towels for comfort. The closer it gets to the whelping, the more time your dog will spend in the whelping box, preparing it for her litter.

During the last week of your Jack Russell Terrier's pregnancy you should start taking her internal temperature at least once per day – this is the greatest indicator of impending labor. The normal body temperature for a dog is about 100°F to 102°F (37.7°C to 38.8°C). When your dog's body temperature drops, you can expect contractions to begin within 24 hours or so. Prior to labor, your dog's body temperature may drop as low as 98°F (36.6°C) – if it gets any lower, contact your veterinarian.

Once your Jack Russell Terrier starts going into labor, you can expect her to show some obvious signs of discomfort. Your dog might start pacing restlessly, panting, and switching positions. The early stages of labor can often last for several hours and contractions may occur as often as 10 minutes apart. If your Jack Russell Terrier has contractions for more than 2 hours without any of the puppies being born, contact your veterinarian immediately. Once your dog starts giving birth, the puppies will arrive about every thirty minutes following ten to thirty minutes of straining.

After each puppy is born, the Jack Russell Terrier will lick the puppy clean; it may even eat the umbilical cord because it is animal instinct. This also helps to stimulate the puppy to start breathing on his own. Once all of the puppies have been born, the mother will expel the rest of the placenta (the afterbirth) and then let the puppies start nursing. It is essential that the puppies begin nursing within one hour of being born because this is when they will receive the colostrum from the mother. Colostrum is the first milk produced and it contains a variety of nutrients as well as antibodies to protect the pups until their own immune systems have time to develop. In addition to making sure that the puppies are feeding, you should also make sure that the mother eats soon after whelping.

Jack Russell Terrier puppies are small in size; these puppies are also born blind, with their eyes and ears closed, so they are completely dependent on the mother for several weeks. Around 3rd week, the puppies will open their eyes and their ears will become erect sometime after. As the puppies grow, they will start to become increasingly active and the will grow very quickly as long as they are properly fed by the mother.

At six weeks of age is the time you should begin weaning the puppies by offering them small amounts of puppy food soaked in water or broth. The puppies might sample small bits of solid food even while they are still nursing and the mother will general wean the puppies by week 8, with or without your help. If you plan to sell the puppies, be sure not to send them home unless they are fully weaned at least 8 weeks old. You should also take steps to start socializing the puppies from an early age to make sure they turn into well-adjusted adults.

Chapter Nine: Keeping Your Dog Healthy

It's your JRT's life – and as a pet owner, your responsibility is to make sure that their life is long, happy and healthy as possible. Are you already prepared to keep you JRTs happy and healthy in a long term? In this section, you will find tons of tips on how to maintain your dog happy and healthy. Information about common health problems is also addressed in this section.

Common Health Problems

Jack Russell Terriers are very healthy, hardy and long-lived type of breed. However, despite this, they still have a relative health issues. The JRT, just like other breeds do have some common health problems. It is important as a pet owner, to be conscientious of your JRT's health at all times, not only when he seems to be not feeling well or has developed an issue. Regular checking your JRTs is a very important step in catching problems early as possible. This applies to JRTs of all ages whether it is puppies, adults or seniors.

Health Issues Seen With the Jack Russell Terrier Breed

The Jack Russell Terrier is also prone to certain canine diseases and health problems just like any other dogs. But this does not mean that your JRT will develop these heath issues. The following are the health problems most common to Jack Russell Terriers.

Hereditary Ataxia

This condition is also called Progressive Ataxia which is inherited via polygenic mode. What happens is that there is a degeneration of nerves which happens in the central nervous system. Because the degeneration does not only happen in one area but all throughout the system, there is a disturbance that happens in the gait. The progression of the disease is very slow and is seen at around the age of -6 months.

The signs and symptoms that your dog may be experiencing this condition are as follows:

- Gait is wobbly
- Goose stepping
- Respiratory distress
- Seizures
- Tremors and shakings

This condition may also affect the dog's nerves which makes the muscles of the spinal cord damaged. Unfortunately, there is no screening that can be done for Hereditary Ataxia. The condition can be observed only when the symptoms become visible. Some who have this condition will not be able to survive up until 2 years of age because they cannot function anymore.

Myasthenia Gravis

Myasthenia Gravis is a not a very prevalent disease in humans but it is a condition also experienced by pets. This condition is characterized by the weakening of the transmission signals of the nerve and muscle. This condition is mostly seen in dogs which are older but can also be seen in the young Jack Russell Terriers. This disease is genetically inherited from a recessive trait.

The primary sign of this condition is the weakening of the muscles. Symptoms are as follows:

- Gets easily tired
- Head hanging in fatigue
- Drooping face
- Walking will be slow
- Having short strides than usual
- Difficulty in swallowing and chewing
- Esophagus not contracting well

Unfortunately, there is no screening for this condition but diagnosis can be done through specialized testing drugs administered by a vet. There is no available treatment for this condition but only pain management and adjustments in food.

Cerebral Ataxis

This condition happens to Jack Russell Terriers at the early age of 2-4 weeks. This is genetically inherited via a recessive trait. The following are the symptoms experienced by your dog if they are suffering from this condition:

- Head bobbing
- In-coordination of movements
- Stumbling and lack of balance
- Wide-based stance
- Inability to stand and walk eventually

Sadly, there is no screening that can be done to detect this condition.

Congestive Heart Failure

This condition is also called Endocardiosis. This is a general condition which affects dogs and particularly the Jack Russell Terrier. This condition greatly affects the function of the valves of the heart.

This condition may cause the valves to be enlarged and may affect the flow of the heart. The blood flow may function backward which causes atrial enlargement, heart murmur and pulmonary congestion. The progression is very slow which causes deformity and deterioration of the valves. Sudden death may be observed. Sadly, there is no available cure for this disease. For treatment, a lifelong medication is required.

Here's how you can detect that your dog has Congestive Heart Failure:

- Annual veterinary examination for characterization of heart murmur and auscultation
- Endocardiography

Cataracts

Canine cataracts are the most common problems affecting the dog's eye. Toy dogs, like the Jack Russell Terrier are more prone to this sickness. This health issue can appear at any age, from when the Jack Russell Terrier is born up until he becomes older, senior dog.

Collapsed Trachea

This is also common to Jack Russell Terrier dogs. Some of this may be because of genetics, but this can be prevented in most cases. The trachea or the windpipe is supported by rings that are made up of cartilage. This cartilage is prone to injury with toy breeds. With regards to trauma related collapsed trachea, it is often due to the use of a collar instead of harness

Skin Problems

Jack Russell Terriers are prone to skin issues. Skin becomes dry and itchy. There are some remedies that can be followed in order to avoid these kinds of health problems.

Distichiasis

This is when eyelashes grow out of place; often nudging into the dog's eye. This should be treated immediately because if this is prolonged, irritation of the lash into the Jack Russell Terrier's eye can actually cause a tear to the cornea.

Entropion

This happens when a dog's eyelid edge rolls inward. This can occur any age and more often than not, this usually happens to the JRT's lower eyelids.

Hypoglycemia

This health issue is usually sudden drop in blood sugar levels. This can be very dangerous and sometimes can be fatal. This commonly happens to puppies under the age of 3 months old.

Luxating Patella

This is an issue affecting the Knee Joint. It can be usually seen in toy breed dogs like the Jack Russell Terrier. This is a condition of a kneecap and can occur because of malformation of the bone from an injury.

Pituitary Dwarfism

This is common to toy breed dogs. It happens when there is a lack of growth hormones in the body. The growth hormones not only affect the growth of a dog, but they also control the condition of the dog's bones, fur and teeth.

Seizures

Any dog may be born with a seizure condition, including a Jack Russell Terrier. It may develop as the dog grows older. It might be scary to watch a JRT go through an episode associated with this.

Skin and coat issues

Allergies can affect at about 20% of all dogs. This can cause skin issues such as peeling, itchy, dry or irritated skin. In some cases, there may be hot spots that lead to the thinning of the hair.

Recommended Vaccinations for Jack Russell Terrier Dogs

All dogs, including Jack Russell Terriers need shots or vaccinations to certain doggy diseases. Your vet will be making a recommendation, but normally, your JRT will get the same thing at the same age as the big dogs.

Puppy shots

Never neglect to get your JRT a shot even it seems that he is too small to have one because this is vital to their health. JRT puppies first get their shots as soon as they leave their mommies. If you get your dog from a breeder at eight to nine weeks old, it is assumed that he already got a shot – even six –week- old puppies can be given a vaccination. When puppies get boosters, they get a natural immunity from their moms but it interferes with the shots that you gave to them. The best thing to do is give your Jack Russell Terrier puppy a series of shots to make sure he's covered when he needs it. Jack Russell Terriers should be getting boosters every two to four weeks until he's 16 weeks old. As soon as he is finished with puppy shots, give your JRTs booster shots once every three years but if your vet recommends annual boosters, follow it and go with that schedule.

Below table summarizes the different vaccinations that can be given to your Jack Russell Terrier. You can review it so you have an idea what shots to give to your dogs.

In this section you will learn the vaccination schedule that your puppy or dog may need, but be sure to consult the veterinarian for further instructions.

Vaccination Schedule for Dogs			
Vaccine	**Doses**	**Age**	**Booster**
Rabies	1	12 weeks	annual
Distemper	3	6-16 weeks	3 years
Parvovirus	3	6-16 weeks	3 years
Adenovirus	3	6-16 weeks	3 years
Parainfluenza	3	6 weeks, 12-14 weeks	3 years
Bordatella	1	6 weeks	annual
Lyme Disease	2	9, 13-14 weeks	annual
Leptospirosis	2	12 and 16 weeks	annual
Canine Influenza	2	6-8, 8-12 weeks	annual

Signs of Possible Illnesses

- **Sneezing** - does your dog have nose discharge?
- **Dehydration** -does your dog drink less than the usual? It may be a sign that there is something wrong with your dog
- **Obesity** -is your dog showing signs of obesity? It may be prone to a heart disease, or diabetes. Monitor your dog's weight before it's too late.
- **Elimination** -does your dog regularly urinate and defecate? Always check its litter to make sure that its stool and urine is normal. Contact the vet immediately if there are any signs of bleed and diarrhea.
- **Vomiting** - does your dog vomits and is it showing signs of appetite loss?
- **Coat** -does its coat and skin still feel soft, firm and rejuvenated? If your dog is sick sometimes, it appears physically on its body.
- **Paws/Limbs** -does your dog have trouble walking or is it only dragging its legs? It could be a sign of paralysis.
- **Eyes** - are there any discharge in the eyes?
- **Overall Physique** - does your dog stays active or are there any signs of weakness and deterioration?

Emergency Guide

Accidents do happen and we cannot avoid them. When there are medical emergencies that befall our dogs, pet parents may find it difficult to make rational decisions, especially when it occurs in the middle of the night. That is why it is very important that we know what to do and should have an emergency plan in place – before we need it.

Signs Your Pet May Need Emergency Care

There are a lot of reasons when your dog needs an emergency care like a severe trauma – caused by accident or fall – choking, insect sting, heatstroke, household poisoning or other life – threatening circumstances. Below are some signs that emergency care is necessary.

- Pale gums
- Rapid breathing
- Weak or rapid pulse
- Change in body temperature
- Difficulty standing
- Apparent paralysis

- Loss of consciousness

- Seizures

- Excessive bleeding

Next steps

Dogs that are severely injured may be aggressive toward their owners, so it is very important to first protect yourself from injury.

Approach your dog calmly and slowly, kneel down and say his name. If the dog is aggressive, call for immediate help. If he is passive, fashion a makeshift stretcher and gently carry him onto it. Be sure to support his neck and back in case he is suffering any spinal injuries.

First Aid Treatments that can be performed at Home

A lot of medical emergencies require immediate veterinary care, but first aid methods may help in stabilizing your pet for transportation.

- If the dog is suffering from bleeding because of trauma, try to elevate and apply pressure to the wound

- If your pet is choking, place your fingers inside his mouth and see if you can remove the blockage

- If you cannot remove the foreign object, perform a modified Heimlich maneuver by giving a sharp rap to his chest, which will dislodge the object.

Performing CPR on your Pet

CPR may be important if your pet remains unconscious after you have removed the object that chokes him. Check first to see if he is still breathing. If not, place him on his side and perform an artificial respiration by extending his neck and head, holding his jaws closed and by blowing into his nostrils once every 3 seconds. Be sure that no air escapes between your mouth and the nose of your pet. If you really cannot hear a heartbeat, incorporate a cardiac massage, while having artificial respiration – three quick, firm chest compression for every respiration until your dog can breath normally already.

What to do if your JRT eats something Poisonous

If you think your JRT has ingested a toxic food or substance, call your vet immediately or the ASPCA Animal Poison Control Center's 24-hour hotline at (888) 426 – 4435. They will make a recommendation, and will consider the age and health of your dog and what and how he ate. This may include inducing vomiting, based on their assessment.

Jack Russell Terrier Care Sheet

You have made it this far! You have all the information that you need into becoming a well-informed dog owner. All the information that you have read will help you in being the best owner that you can be for your new pet. I'm sure you are excited for the next chapter of your life after reading this book—becoming an official pet owner!

This chapter contains a summary of everything that you have read and learned from this book.

Jack Russell Terrier Information Sheet

Pedigree: Jack Russell Terrier Club of America

AKC Group: Terrier

Breed Size: Small

Height: 10-15 inches (25-38 cm) tall

Weight: weighs 6-8 kg

Coat Texture: may be smooth, broken, or rough

Color: white should be the dominant color with tan or black markings (from chestnut tan to the lightest shade of tan); can also appear as tricolor having consistent patches

Eyes: small almond eyes that is dark and expressive

Ears: button, drop ears should be falling forward

Tail: erect when moving and dropping when at rest; 4-5 inches in length

Temperament: can be easily trained, intelligent, brave, agile, active, obedient,

Strangers: sociable when trained well

Other Dogs: good with proper socialization but may have barking tendencies because of his hunting instincts

Other Pets: generally not good with other pets

Training: Highly trainable

Exercise Needs: requires a lot of exercise and play time with the use of lively activities; about 40 minutes a day

Health Conditions: generally healthy but may be prone to certain health conditions such as Cataracts, Glaucoma, Luxating Patella, Hereditary ataxia, Legg-Calve-Perthes Disease, Cerebral Ataxia, Congestive Heart Failure, Myasthenia Gravis, Pituitary Dwarfism etc.

Lifespan: average 13-16 years or more

Jack Russell Terrier's Habitat Requirements

Recommended Accessories: dog bed, food/water dishes, toys, collar, leash, harness, grooming supplies

Collar and Harness: size by weight

Grooming: brush coat everyday

Energy Level: high energy level

Exercise Requirements: 40 minutes a day of training, walking and playing

Food/Water: uses stainless steel or ceramic bowls, clean daily

Toys: start with an assortment to check which the dog likes

Jack Russell Terrier's Nutritional Needs

Nutritional Needs: water, protein, carbohydrate, fats, vitamins, minerals

Important Ingredients: fresh animal protein (chicken, beef, lamb, turkey, eggs), digestible carbohydrates (rice, oats, barley), animal fats

Important Minerals: calcium, phosphorus, potassium, magnesium, iron, copper and manganese

Important Vitamins: Vitamin A, Vitamin A, Vitamin B-12, Vitamin D, Vitamin C

Look For: AAFCO statement of nutritional adequacy; protein at top of ingredients list; no artificial flavors, dyes, preservatives

Breeding Information

Age of First Heat: 6 months old, sometimes earlier or later by a few months

Heat (Estrus) Cycle: 14 to 21 days

Frequency: twice a year, every 5 to 7 months

Greatest Fertility: 11 to 15 days into the cycle

Gestation Period: 59 to 63 days

Pregnancy Detection: possible after 21 days, best to wait 28-30 days before exam

Puppies: born with eyes and ears closed; eyes open at 3 weeks, teeth develop at 10 weeks

Litter Size: average of 3 puppies

Size at Birth: about 6- 6 ½ oz.

Weaning: supplement with controlled portions of moistened puppy food at around 4 weeks, or when the mother starts losing interest in feeding the puppies. Fully weaned at 7-8 weeks

Socialization: start as early as possible to prevent puppies from being nervous as an adult, preferably before 14-16 weeks of age

Index

C

D

H

I

K

L

Photo Credits

Introduction Photo by kkolosov via Pixabay

<https://pixabay.com/photo-2029214/>

Chapter 1 Photo by Alexas_Fotos via Pixabay

<https://pixabay.com/photo-1034737/>

Chapter 2 Photo by coyot via Pixabay

<https://pixabay.com/photo-1653836/>

Chapter 3 Photo by PublicDomainPictures / 18043 images via Pixabay

<https://pixabay.com/photo-69394/>

Chapter 4 Photo by Kdsphotos via Pixabay

<https://pixabay.com/photo-1591145/>

Chapter 5 Photo by Kdsphotos via Pixabay

<https://pixabay.com/photo-1591144/>

Chapter 6 Photo by PublicDomainPictures / 18042 images

< https://pixabay.com/photo-216116/>

Chapter 7 Photo by ASSY via Pixabay

<https://pixabay.com/photo-1731500/>

Chapter 8 Photo by Yolanda via Pixabay

<https://pixabay.com/photo-503563/>

Chapter 9 Photo by skeeze via Pixabay

<https://pixabay.com/photo-750764/>

Chapter 10 Photo by GeorgeCinna via Pixabay

<https://pixabay.com/photo-578043/>

Care Sheet Photo by Nataaliaml via Pixabay

<https://pixabay.com/photo-1912449/>

References

"Addison's Disease in Dogs." PetMD.

<http://www.petmd.com/dog/conditions/endocrine/c_dg_hy poadrenocorticism>

"Ask a Vet: Are the Small Lumps on My Dog's Skin Serious?" Washingtonian Staff

<https://www.washingtonian.com/2014/12/10/ask-a-vet-are-the-lumps-on-my-dog-serious/>

"Bleeding Disorder in Dogs." PetMD.

<http://www.petmd.com/dog/conditions/cardiovascular/c_dg_von_willebrand_disease>>

"Breeding Jack Russell Terriers"
<http://www.therealjackrussell.com/advice/breed.php>

"Cataracts in Dogs."PetMD.

<http://www.petmd.com/dog/conditions/eye/c_dg_cataract>

"Crate Training."American Dog Trainers Network.

<http://inch.com/~dogs/cratetraining.html>

"Dog Behavior Training – Proven Techniques to Help Solve Problem Behaviors. Dog Training Central.

<http://www.dog-obedience-training-review.com/dog-behavior-training.html>

"Dog Nutrition Tips." ASPCA.

<http://www.aspca.org/pet-care/dog-care/dog-nutrition-tips>

"Epilepsy in a Poodle." Francine Richards.

<http://pets.thenest.com/epilepsy-poodle-6105.html>

"Estrus Cycle in Dogs."VCA.

<http://www.vcahospitals.com/main/pet-health-information/article/animal-health/estrus-cycles-in-dogs/5778>

"Feeding Dogs: Guide to the Small Dog Diet." Small Dog Place.

<http://www.smalldogplace.com/feeding-dogs.html>

"General Poodle Information."The Pampered Poodle Palace.

<http://www.thepamperedpoodlepalace.com/cratetrainingcare.htm>

"Genetic Welfare Problems of Companion Animals."UFAW.

<http://www.ufaw.org.uk/dogs/poodle---hereditary-cataract>

"Getting Started Showing Your Dog."AKC.

<http://www.akc.org/events/conformation-dog-
    shows/getting-started-showing/>

"Glaucoma in Dogs."PetMD.

<http://www.petmd.com/dog/conditions/eyes/c_dg_glauco
    ma>

"Glaucoma in Dogs." Vetary.com.
<https://www.vetary.com/dog/condition/glaucoma>

"Housebreaking (Potty Training) for Puppies and Adult
Dogs." Michele Welton.
<http://www.yourpurebredpuppy.com/training/articles/do
g-housebreaking.html>

"How to Break 7 Common Bad Dog Habits." Shayna
    Meliker. VetStreet.

<http://www.vetstreet.com/our-pet-experts/how-to-break-7-
    common-bad-dog-habits>

"How to Choose a Good Puppy (Picking the Best Puppy in a
Litter)." Michele Welton.
<http://www.yourpurebredpuppy.com/buying/articles/how-
to-choose-a-puppy.html>

"How to Choose an Experienced Dog Breeder."PetMD.

<http://www.petmd.com/dog/care/evr_dg_breeders>

"How to Choose High-Quality Dog Food."Alphadog.

<https://alphadogfood.com/choose-high-quality-dog-food>

"How to Find a Responsible Dog Breeder."The Humane Society of the United States.
<http://www.humanesociety.org/issues/puppy_mills/tips/finding_responsible_dog_breeder.html?referrer=https://www.google.com/>

"How to Prevent Tear Stains on Your Dog's Face." AKC.
<http://www.akc.org/content/dog-care/articles/tear-stains/>

"Hypoglycemia – Low Blood Sugar." Douglas Brum, DVM. <http://www.canine-epilepsy-guardian-angels.com/hypoglycemia.htm>

"Inflammatory Skin Disease in Dogs."PetMD.
<http://www.petmd.com/dog/conditions/skin/c_dg_sebaceous_adenitis>

"Intervertebral Disk Disease (IVDD)."ExpertVet.
<http://www.expertvet.com/articles/intervertebral-disk-disease-ivdd>

"Jack Russell Terrier; Russell Terrier, JRT, and Jack" GRAPHIQ.
<http://dogs.petbreeds.com/l/196/Jack-Russell-Terrier>

"Jack Russell Terrier Temperament". Michele Welton. <www.yourpurebredpuppy.com/reviews/jackrussell>

"Jack Russell Terrier Dog Breed Information and Personality Traits"

<www.hillspet.com/en/us/dog-breeds/jack-russell-terrier>

"Keeping Your Puppy Safe at Home." Erin Ollila. <http://www.hillspet.com/en/us/dog-care/new-pet-parent/puppy-proofing-your-home>

"Knee Problems in Your Dog: Patellar Luxation – Luxating Kneecaps." 2ndchance.info./Ronald Hines. <http://www.2ndchance.info/patella.htm>

"Legg-Calve-Perthes disease."UPEI.

<http://discoveryspace.upei.ca/cidd/disorder/legg-calvé-perthes-disease>

"Legg-Calve-Perthes Disease in Dogs."PetMD.

<http://www.petmd.com/dog/conditions/musculoskeletal/c_dg_legg_calve_perthes_disease>

"Luxating Patella." Race Foster, DVM. <http://www.peteducation.com/article.cfm?c=2+2084&aid=457>

"New to Dog Showing?" The Kennel Club.

<http://www.thekennelclub.org.uk/activities/dog-showing/new-to-dog-showing/>

"Optic Nerve Hypoplasia." Go Pets America. <http://www.gopetsamerica.com/dog-health/optic-nerve-hypoplasia.aspx>

"Optic Nerve Hypoplasia." Vetbook.org. <http://www.vetbook.org/wiki/dog/index.php?title=Optic_nerve_hypoplasia>

"Owning a Dog Cost."Costhelper.

<http://pets.costhelper.com/owning-dog.html>

"People Foods to Avoid Feeding Your Pets."ASPCA.

<http://www.aspca.org/pet-care/animal-poison-control/people-foods-avoid-feeding-your-pets>

"Preparing for a dog show."Your Dog. <http://www.yourdog.co.uk/Dog-Activities/preparing-for-a-dog-show.html>

"Progressive Retinal Atrophy (PRA)."Davies Veterinary Specialists.

<http://vetspecialists.co.uk/factsheets/Ophthalmology_Facts/Progressive_Retinal_Atrophy.html>

"Puppy proofing basics." Wendy Wilson. <https://www.cesarsway.com/dog-care/puppies/puppy-proofing-basics>

"Registered Standard Poodles with Addison's Disease (Hypoadrenocorticism)."Poodle Health Registry.

<http://www.poodlehealthregistry.org/docs/Standard/PHR_Standard_Addison.html>

"Responsible Breeding."AKC.

<http://www.akc.org/dog-breeders/responsible-breeding/>

"Routine Vaccinations for Puppies and Dogs."WebMD.

<http://pets.webmd.com/dogs/guide/routine-vaccinations-puppies-dogs>

"Seizures in Dogs." Thomas K. Graves, DVM.
<http://www.canine-epilepsy.com/Graves.html>

"Skin Tumors in Dogs (Benign & Malignant)."PetWave.

<http://www.petwave.com/Dogs/Health/Skin-Tumors.aspx>

"Sleeping Arrangement for New Puppy."BFF Dog Training LLC.

<http://www.bfftraining.com/available-puppies/puppy-behavior-problems/sleeping-arrangement-for-new-puppy/>

"Socializing Your Dog." Le poodles guide.

<http://www.le-poodles-guide.com/socializing-your-dog.html>

"Socializing Your Puppy or Adult Dog To Get Along With The World." Michele Welton. <http://www.yourpurebredpuppy.com/training/articles/dog-socializing.html>

"Symptoms of Intervertebral Disc Disease in Dogs."PetWave.

<http://www.petwave.com/Dogs/Health/Intervertebral-Disk-Disease/Symptoms.aspx>

"Ten Tips for Showing Your Dog." Kelly Roper. <http://dogs.lovetoknow.com/dog-information/ten-tips-showing-your-dog>

"The Hidden Message Behind Your Pet's Tear Stains." Dr. Karen Becker. <http://healthypets.mercola.com/sites/healthypets/archive/2014/11/12/pet-tear-staining.aspx>

"The Stages of Puppy Growth." Josh Weiss-Roessler. <https://www.cesarsway.com/dog-behavior/puppies/the-stages-of-puppy-growth-and-development>

"Thinking of Buying a Puppy? Find a Responsible Breeder." AKC.

<http://www.akc.org/press-center/facts-stats/responsible-breeders/>

"Tips for Choosing a Healthy Puppy." Susan Koranki. <http://www.fidosavvy.com/choosing-a-healthy-puppy.html>

"Tracheal Collapse in Dogs."WebMD.

<http://pets.webmd.com/dogs/tracheal-collapse-dogs>

"Treatment Options For Your Dog's Luxating Patella." Dr. Julie Mayer. <http://www.dogsnaturallymagazine.com/treatment-options-for-the-luxating-patella/>

"Understanding Bloat and Torsion."Kifka Borzoi. <http://www.kifka.com/Elektrik/Bloat.htm>

"Vaccinations For Your Pet." ASPCA.

<http://www.aspca.org/pet-care/general-pet-care/vaccinations-your-pet>

"Vaccination Schedule for Dogs and Puppies."PetEducation.

<http://www.peteducation.com/article.cfm?c=2+2115&aid=950>

"Vaccinating Your Pet."RSPCA.

<https://www.rspca.org.uk/adviceandwelfare/pets/general/vaccinating>

"Want to Do Well at the Dog Show? Prepare All You Can Ahead of Time." AKC.

<http://www.akc.org/content/dog-training/articles/prepare-ahead-of-time/>

"Weaning Puppies." Race Foster, DVM.
<http://www.peteducation.com/article.cfm?c=2+1651&aid=887>

"Weaning Puppies from their Mother."PetMD.

<http://www.petmd.com/dog/puppycenter/nutrition/evr_dg_weaning_puppies_from_their_mother#>

"Weaning Puppies: What to Do."WebMD.

<http://pets.webmd.com/dogs/weaning-puppies-what-do>

"What to Do Quickly if Your Pet Stars Limping." Dr. Karen Becker.
<http://healthypets.mercola.com/sites/healthypets/archive/2015/01/04/legg-calve-perthes-disease.aspx>

"What You Need to Know About Collapsing Tracheas in Dogs." Dr. Donna Spector, DVM, DACVIM.
<http://www.vetstreet.com/our-pet-experts/what-you-need-to-know-about-collapsing-tracheas-in-dogs>

"Where Should My Puppy Sleep?" Katarina.

<http://doglifetraining.com/2012/08/where-should-my-puppy-sleep/

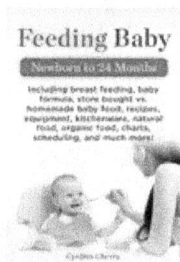

Feeding Baby
Cynthia Cherry
978-1941070000

Axolotl
Lolly Brown
978-0989658430

Dysautonomia, POTS
Syndrome
Frederick Earlstein
978-0989658485

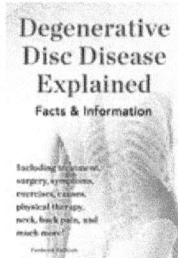

Degenerative Disc
Disease Explained
Frederick Earlstein
978-0989658485

Sinusitis, Hay Fever,
Allergic Rhinitis Explained
Frederick Earlstein
978-1941070024

Wicca
Riley Star
978-1941070130

Zombie Apocalypse
Rex Cutty
978-1941070154

Capybara
Lolly Brown
978-1941070062

Eels As Pets
Lolly Brown
978-1941070167

Scabies and Lice Explained
Frederick Earlstein
978-1941070017

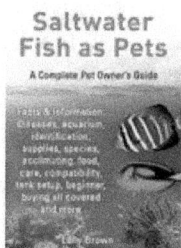

Saltwater Fish As Pets
Lolly Brown
978-0989658461

Torticollis Explained
Frederick Earlstein
978-1941070055

Kennel Cough
Lolly Brown
978-0989658409

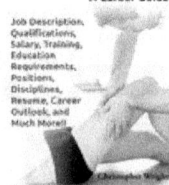

Physiotherapist, Physical Therapist
Christopher Wright
978-0989658492

Rats, Mice, and Dormice As Pets
Lolly Brown
978-1941070079

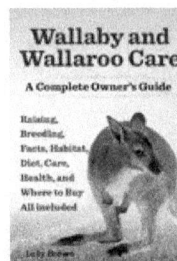

Wallaby and Wallaroo Care
Lolly Brown
978-1941070031

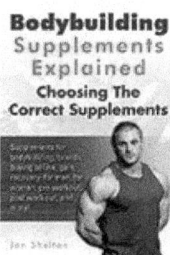

Bodybuilding Supplements
Explained
Jon Shelton
978-1941070239

Demonology
Riley Star
978-19401070314

Pigeon Racing
Lolly Brown
978-1941070307

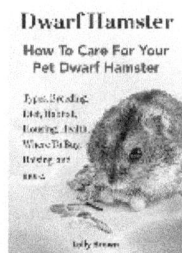

Dwarf Hamster
Lolly Brown
978-1941070390

Cryptozoology
Rex Cutty
978-1941070406

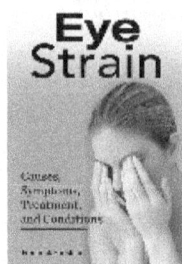

Eye Strain
Frederick Earlstein
978-1941070369

Inez The Miniature Elephant
Asher Ray
978-1941070353

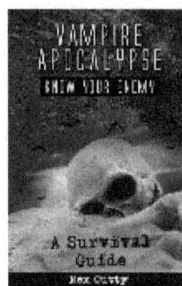

Vampire Apocalypse
Rex Cutty
978-1941070321